Don't Trash it! Reduce, Reuse, and Recycle!
Conservation for Kids
Children's Conservation Books

PROFESSOR GUSTO
EDUCATIONAL & INFORMATIVE BOOKS FOR CHILDREN
(PRE-K / K-12)

Copyright 2016

All Rights reserved. No part of this book may be reproduced or used in any way or form or by any means whether electronic or mechanical, this means that you cannot record or photocopy any material ideas or tips that are provided in this book

Are you familiar with the three Rs? Kids, lets reduce, reuse and recycle!

Let's take a look at proper waste management for happy living. Here are some great ways to eliminate waste. Let's join hands and protect our environment.

Reduce

UCE

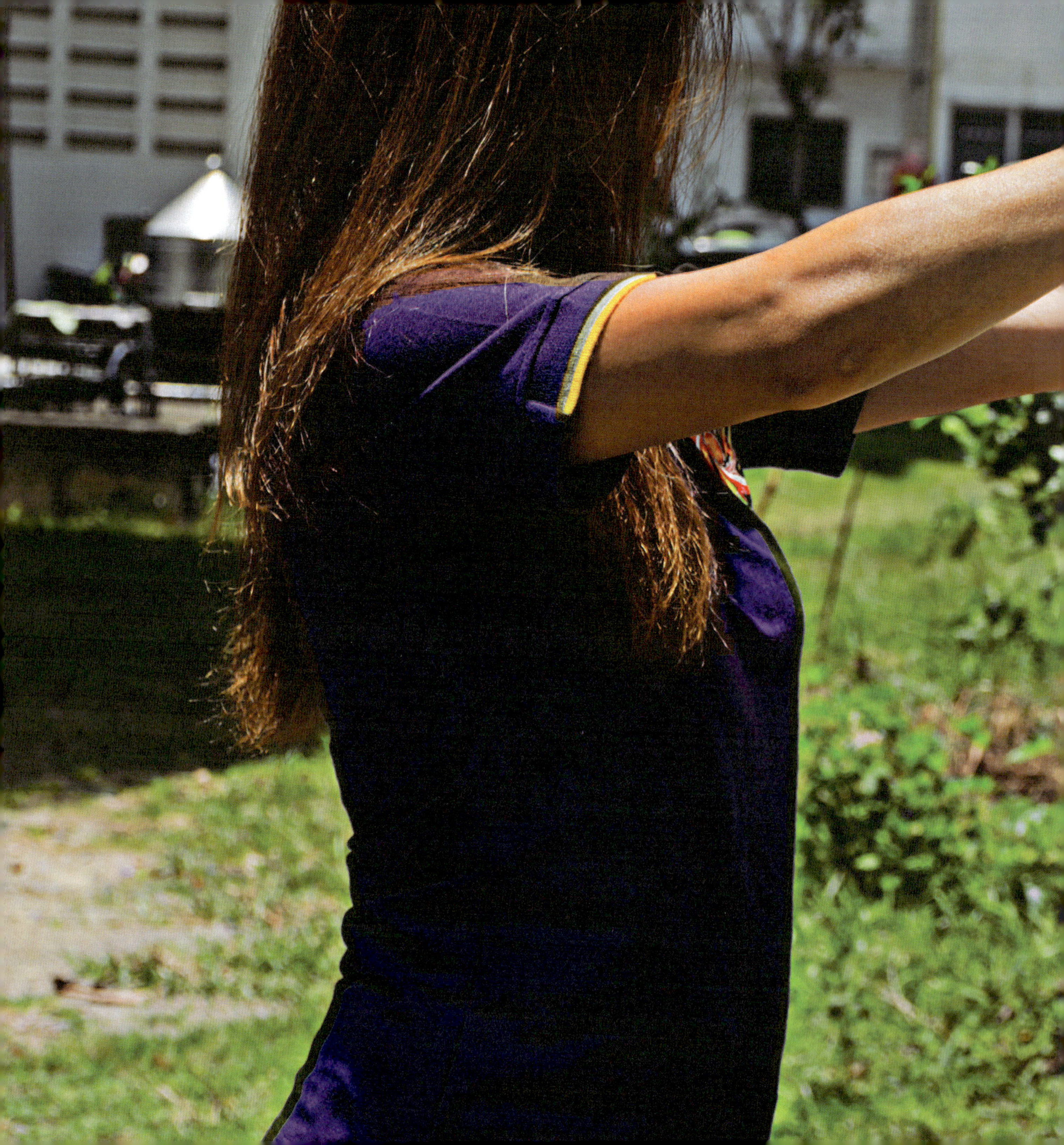

We should avoid producing waste. It's a good way of helping the environment. Would this be possible? This can be done by buying thoughtfully, and only buying what we need.

Avoid buying products that are wrapped in many layers of plastic or foam packing.

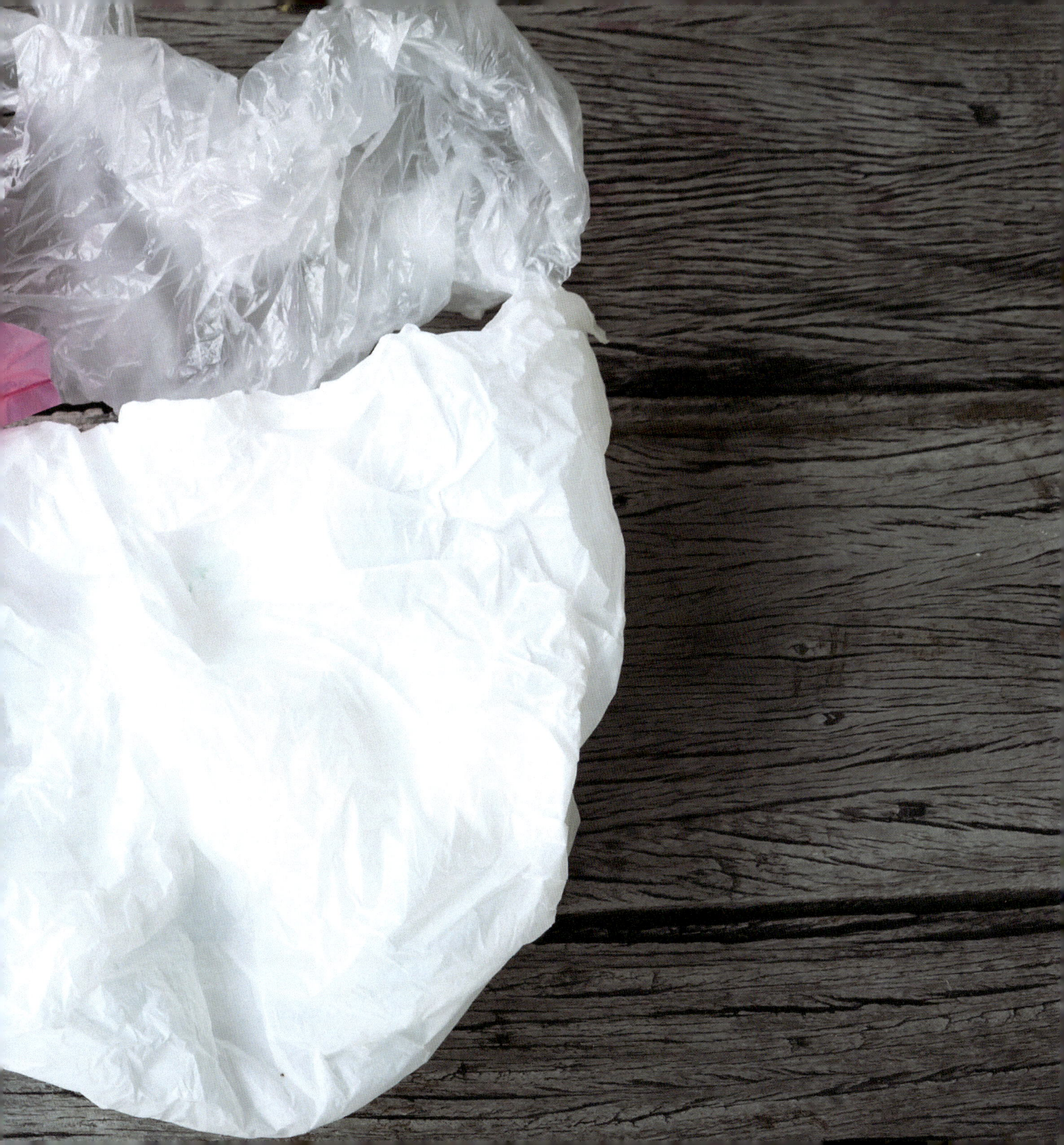

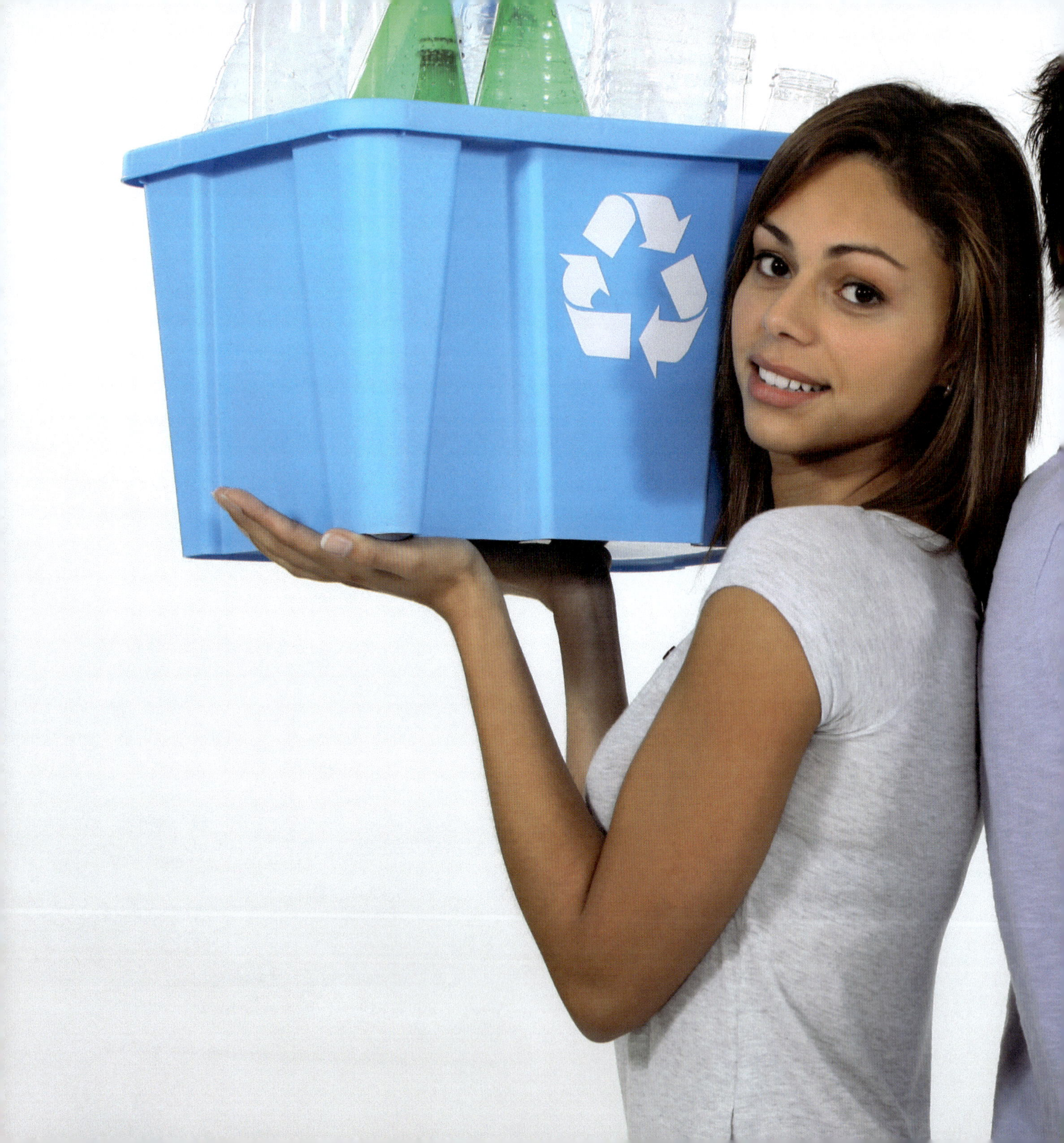

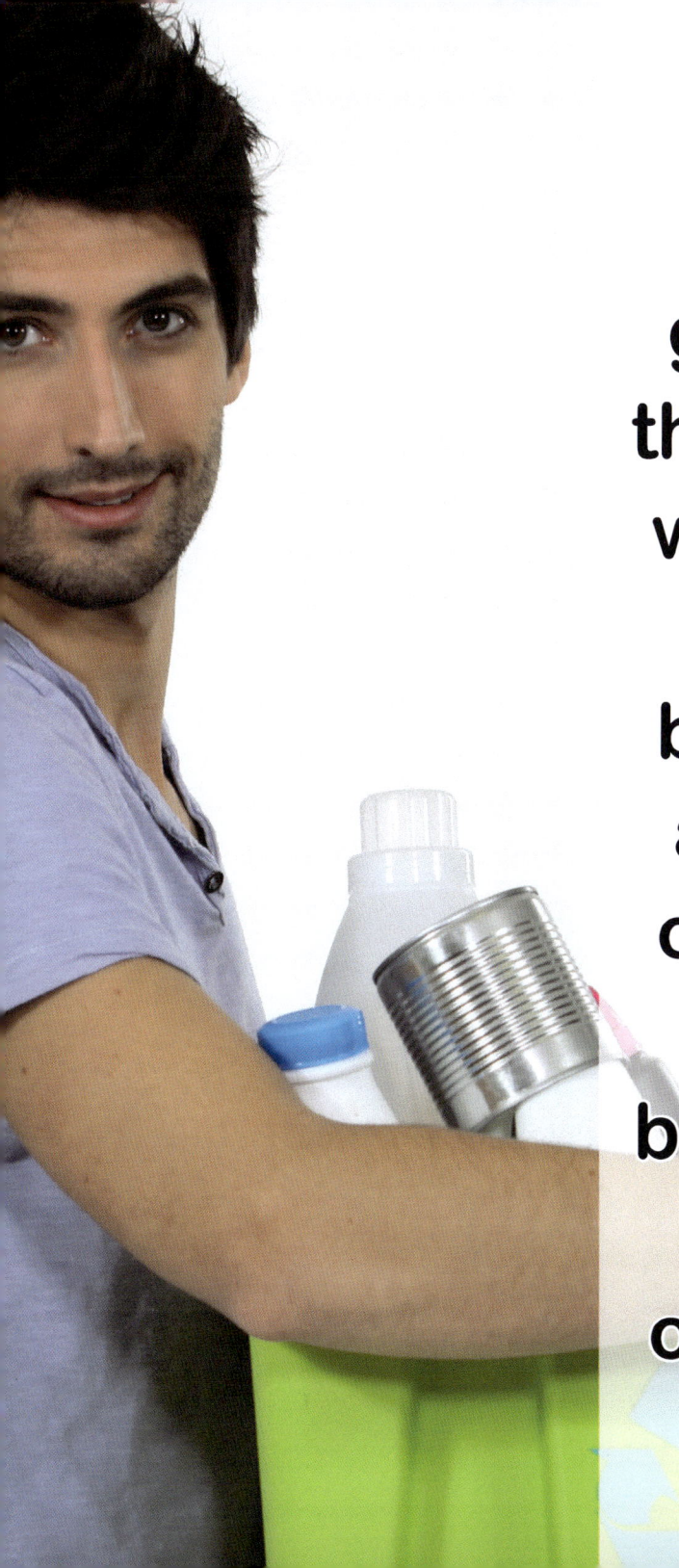

If you are only going to use the thing once, or just want to try it out, see if you can borrow one from a friend instead of buying it right away. Avoid buying something new if you will only use it rarely.

Walk or ride your bike instead of driving.

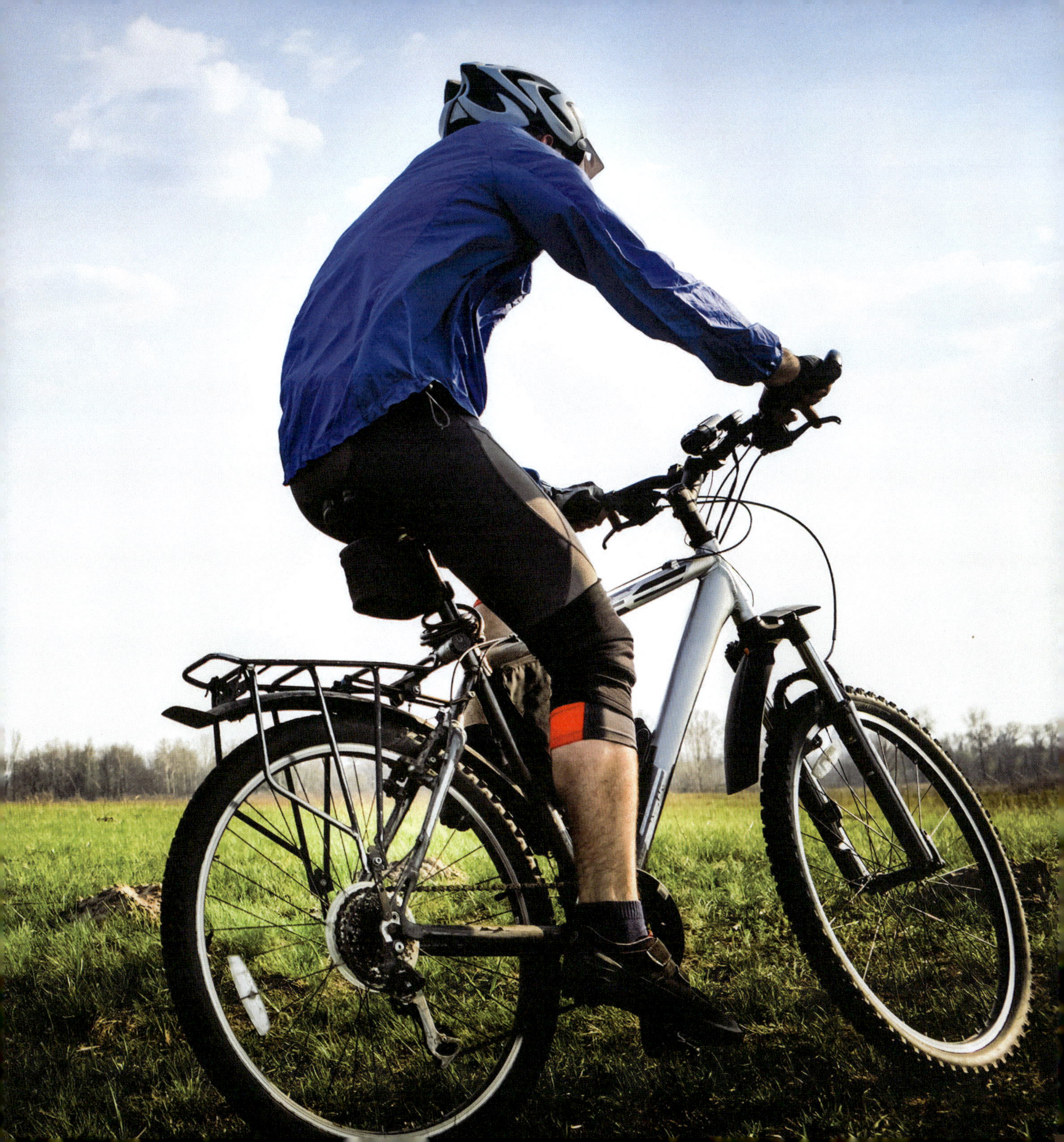

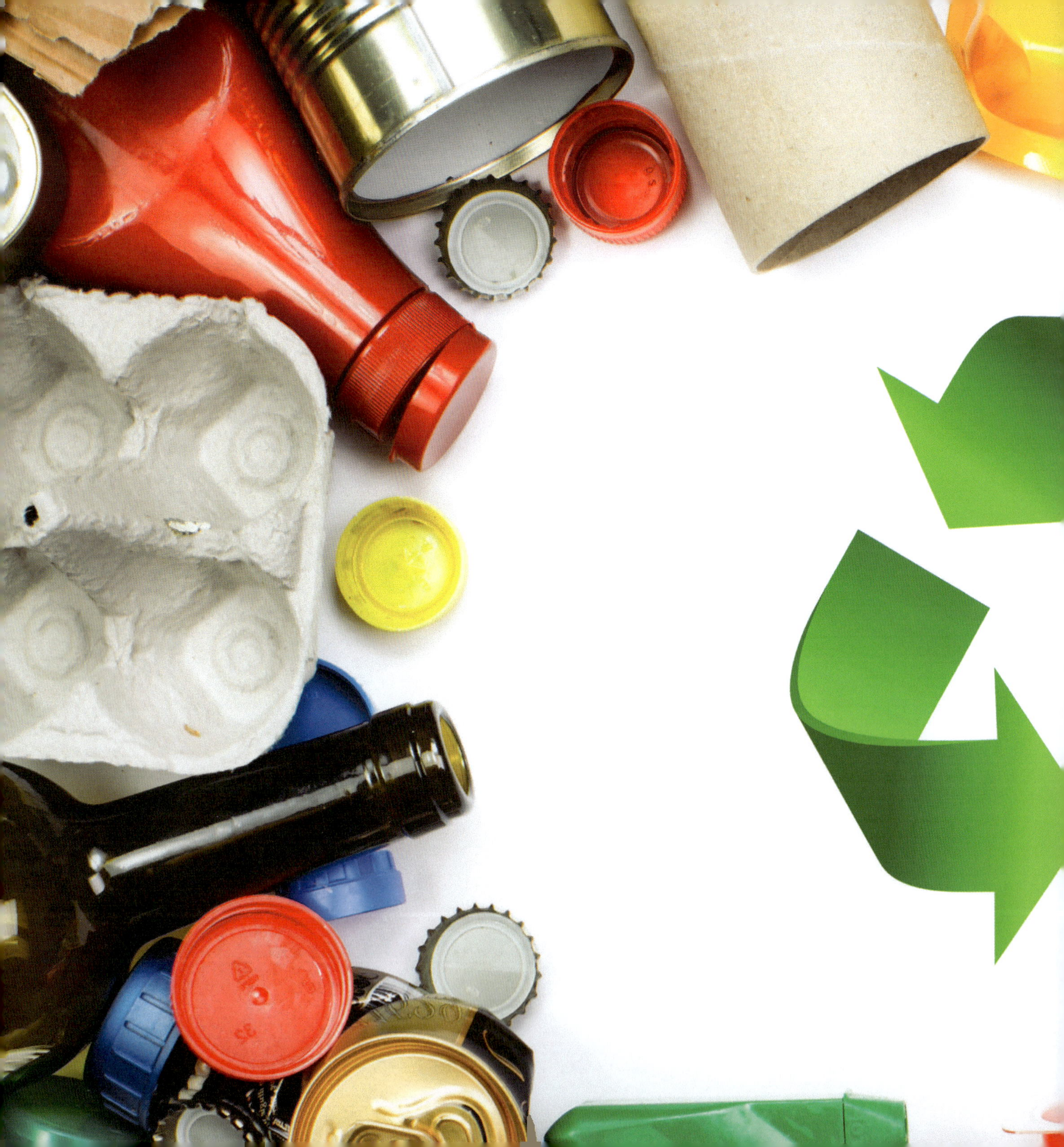

Reuse

Reusing products sounds economical and environment-friendly. It just takes a little creativity.

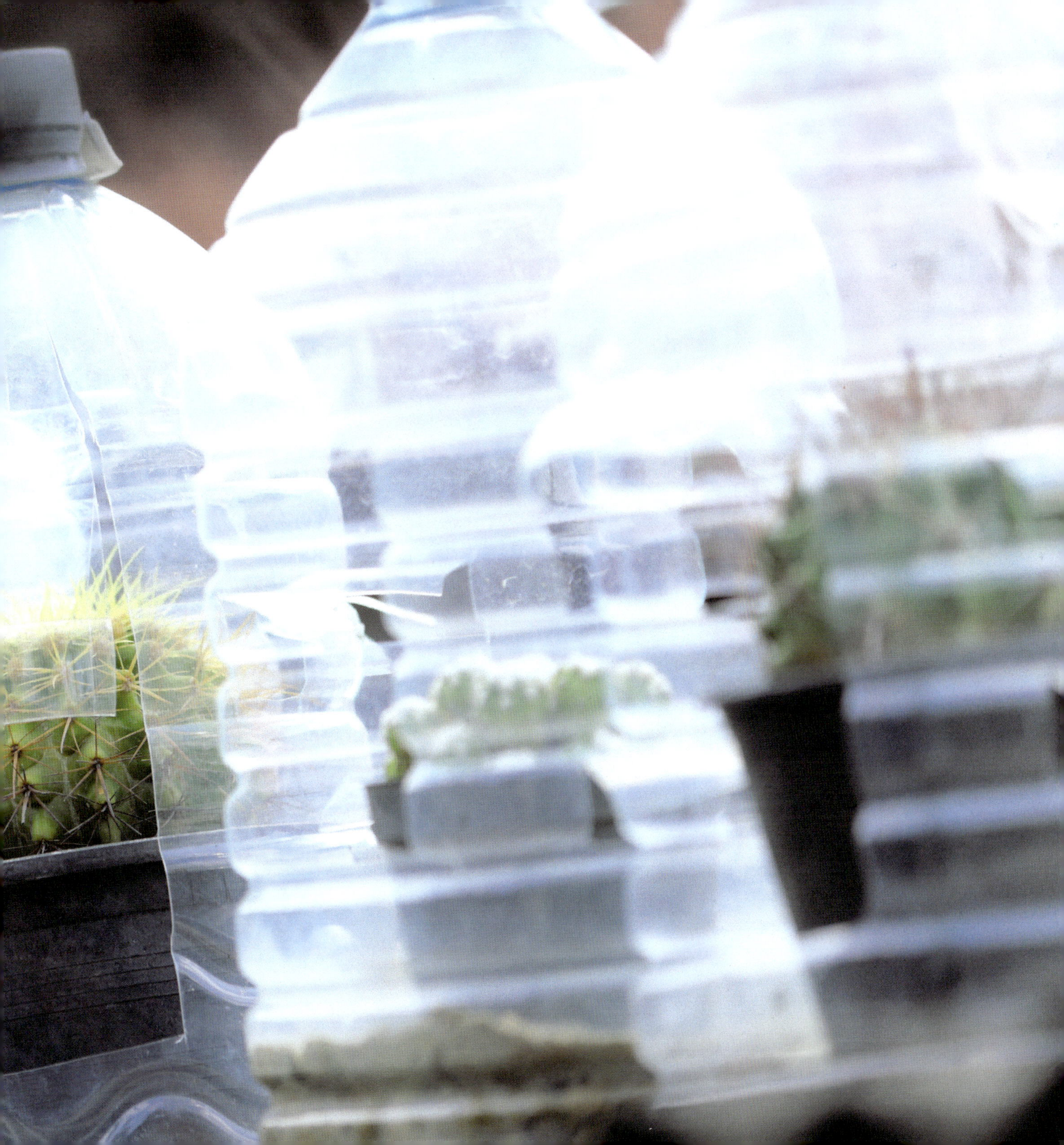

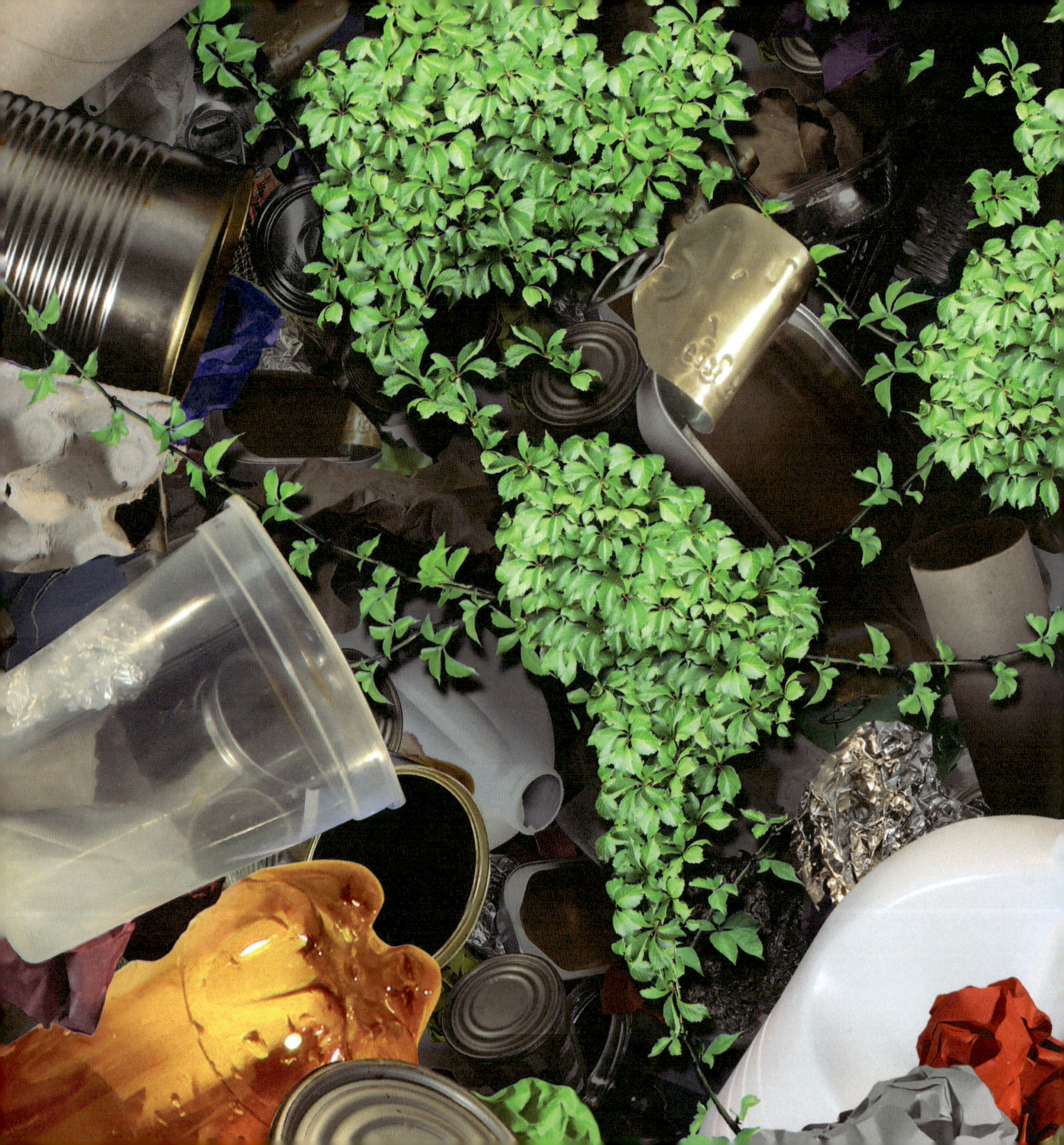

Your trash could be a treasure to someone else. Why not donate the things that you don't need any more? Donate your unwanted appliances and other goods to help others in need.

Reuse products like paper and plastic bags. Repair appliances or tools, if you can, instead of buying brand-new ones.

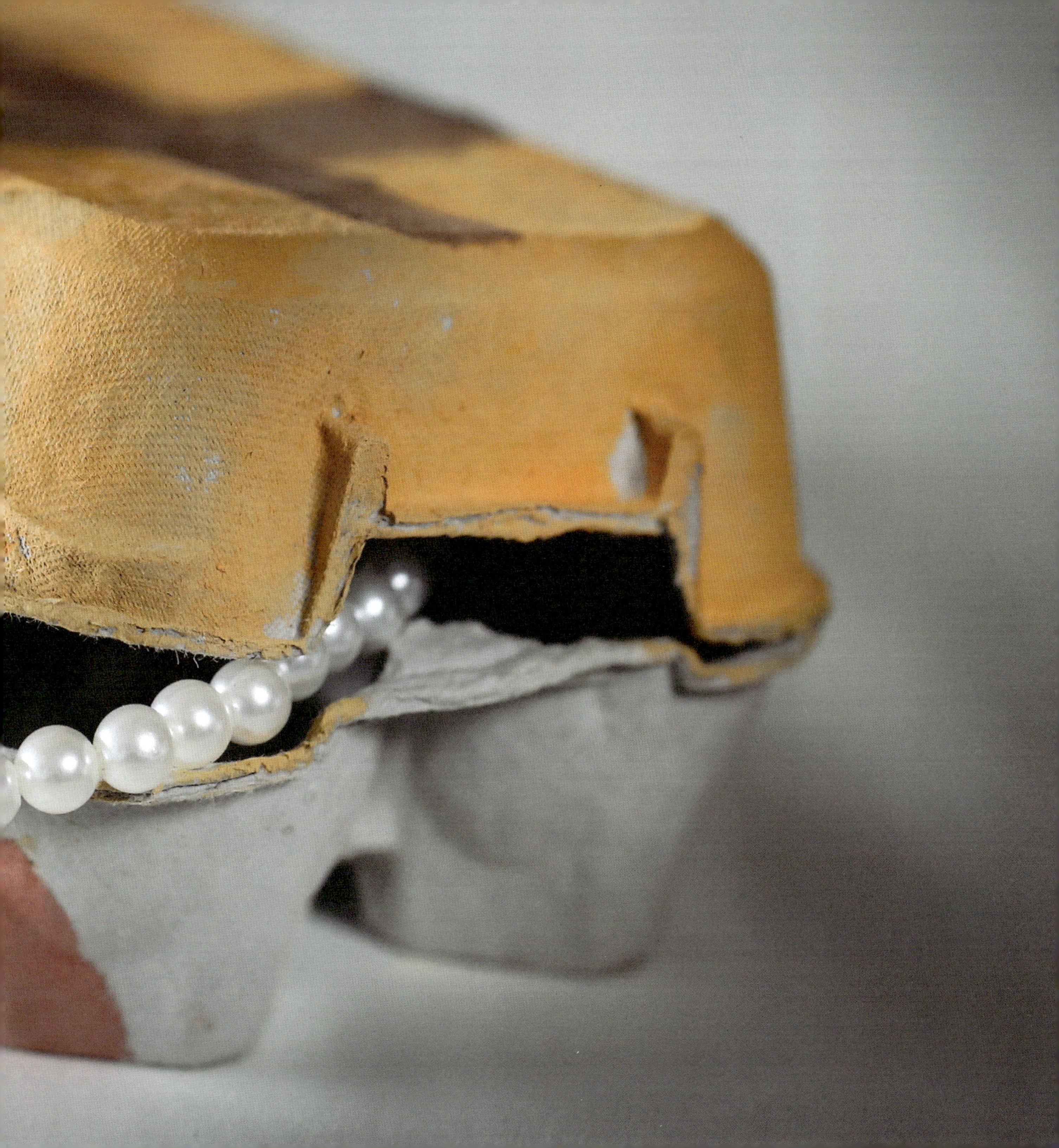

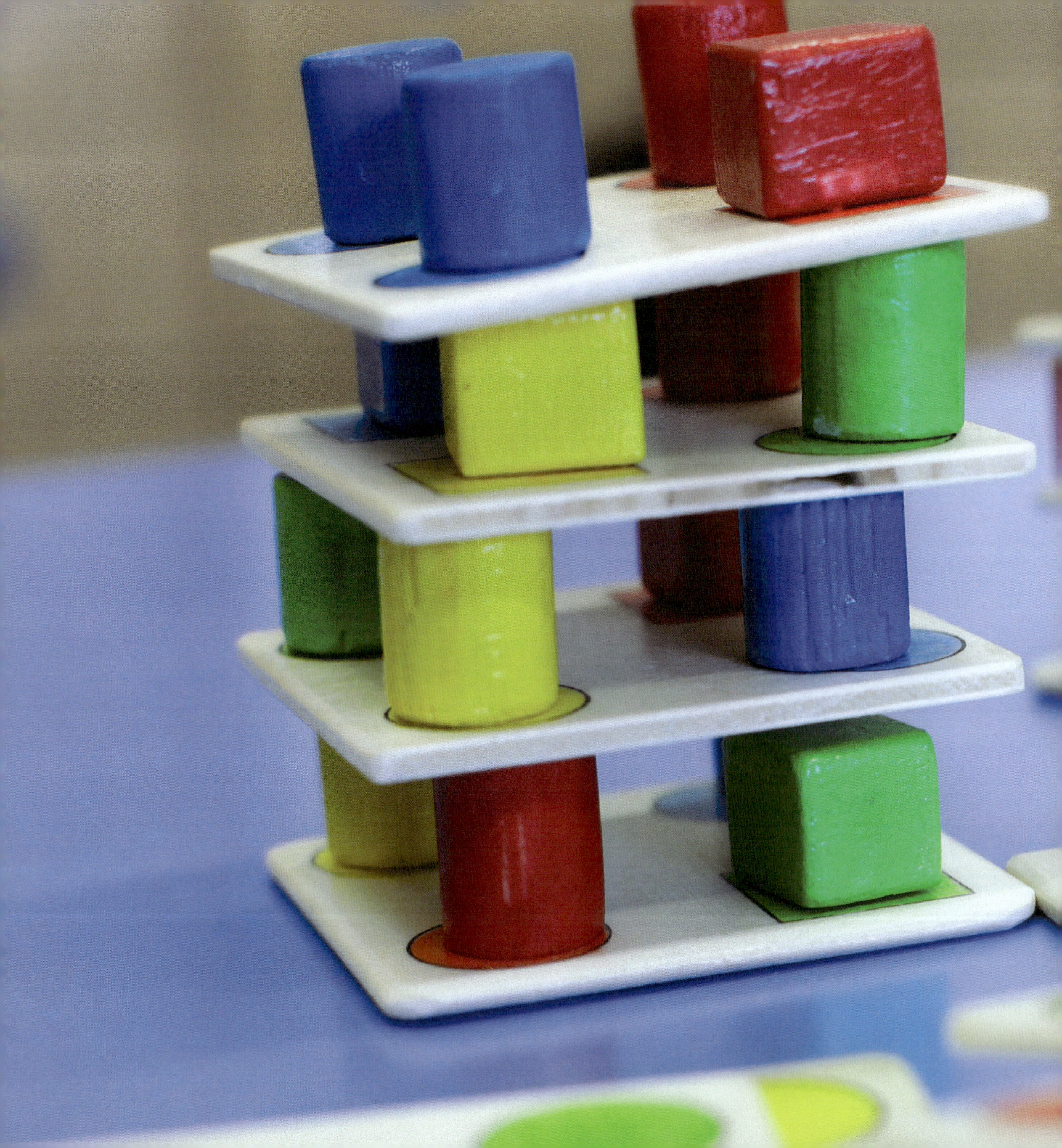

We can reuse products for different ways. Our creativity matters. Microwave trays can be used us picnic dishes.

Recycle

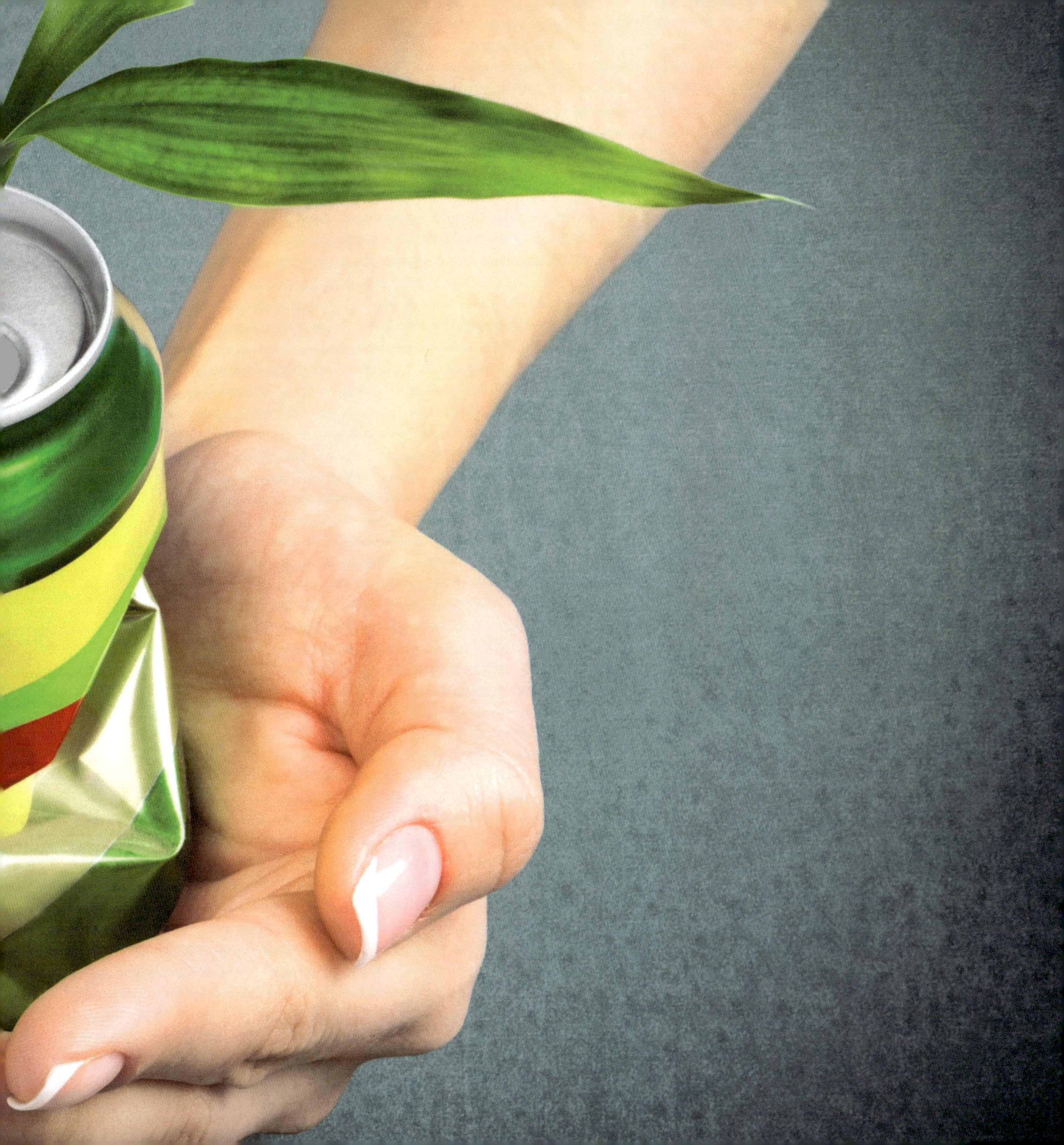

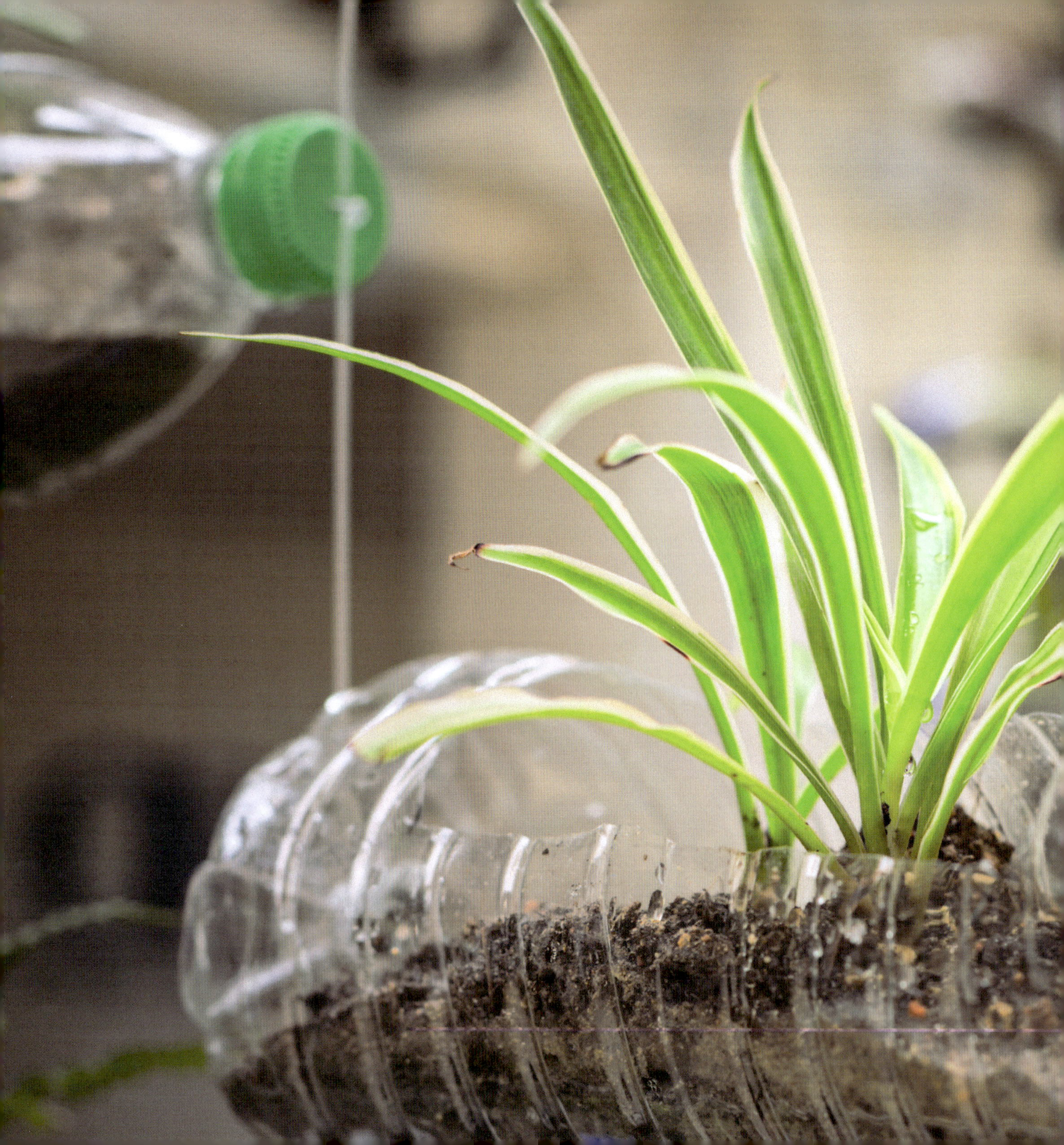

Recycling is making a new product from parts of an old product. Recycling involves many steps. If you like what you're doing, you might as well enjoy doing it. Just think of how you are protecting the environment, then recycling can be a fun activity.

The things we use every day like soda cans, milk boxes, paper bags, and bottles are waste materials that can be recycled, not put in a landfill.

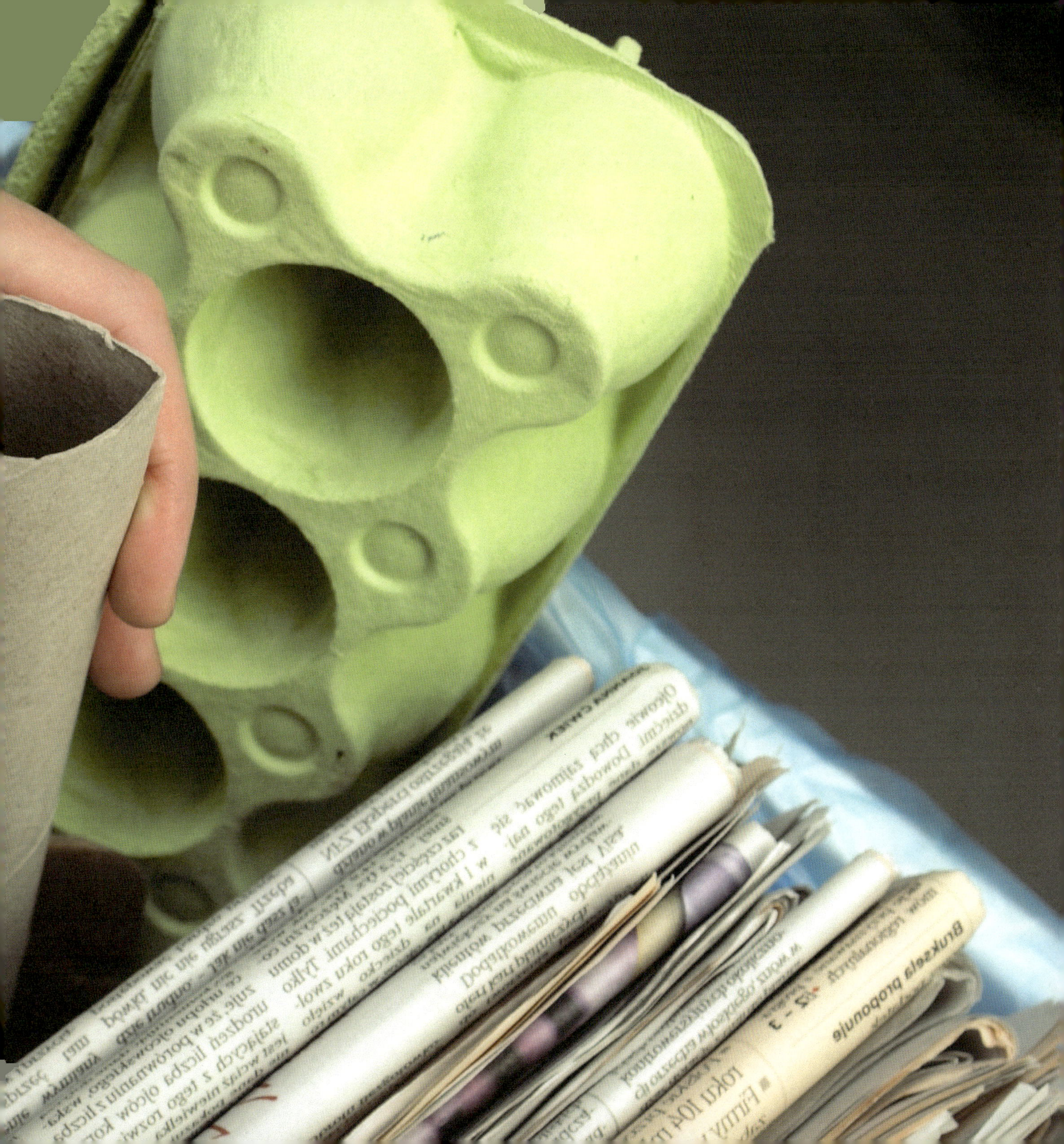

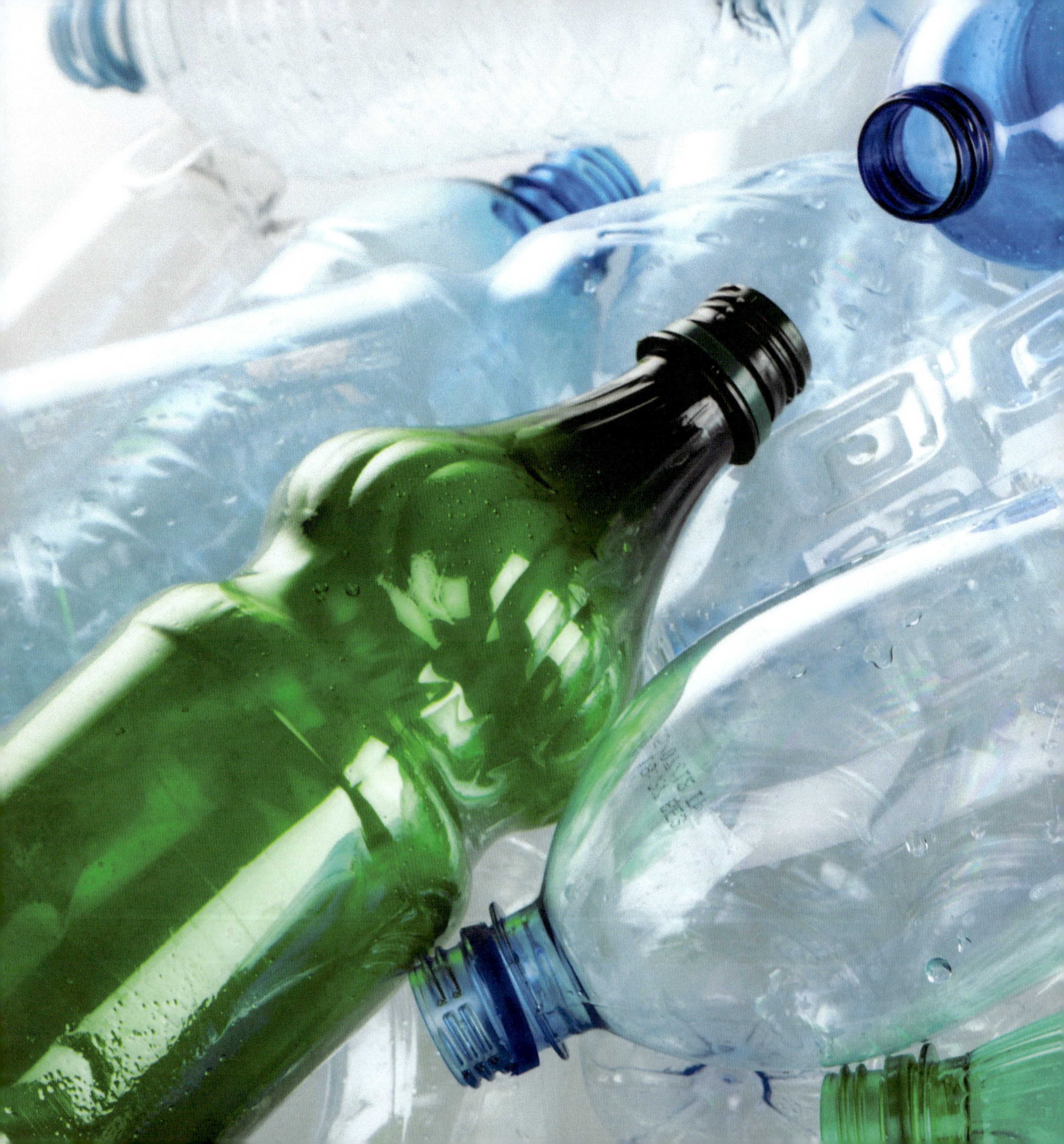

Try to create new products out of these materials.

If you're not that creative, you can give your materials to centers that will recycle things.

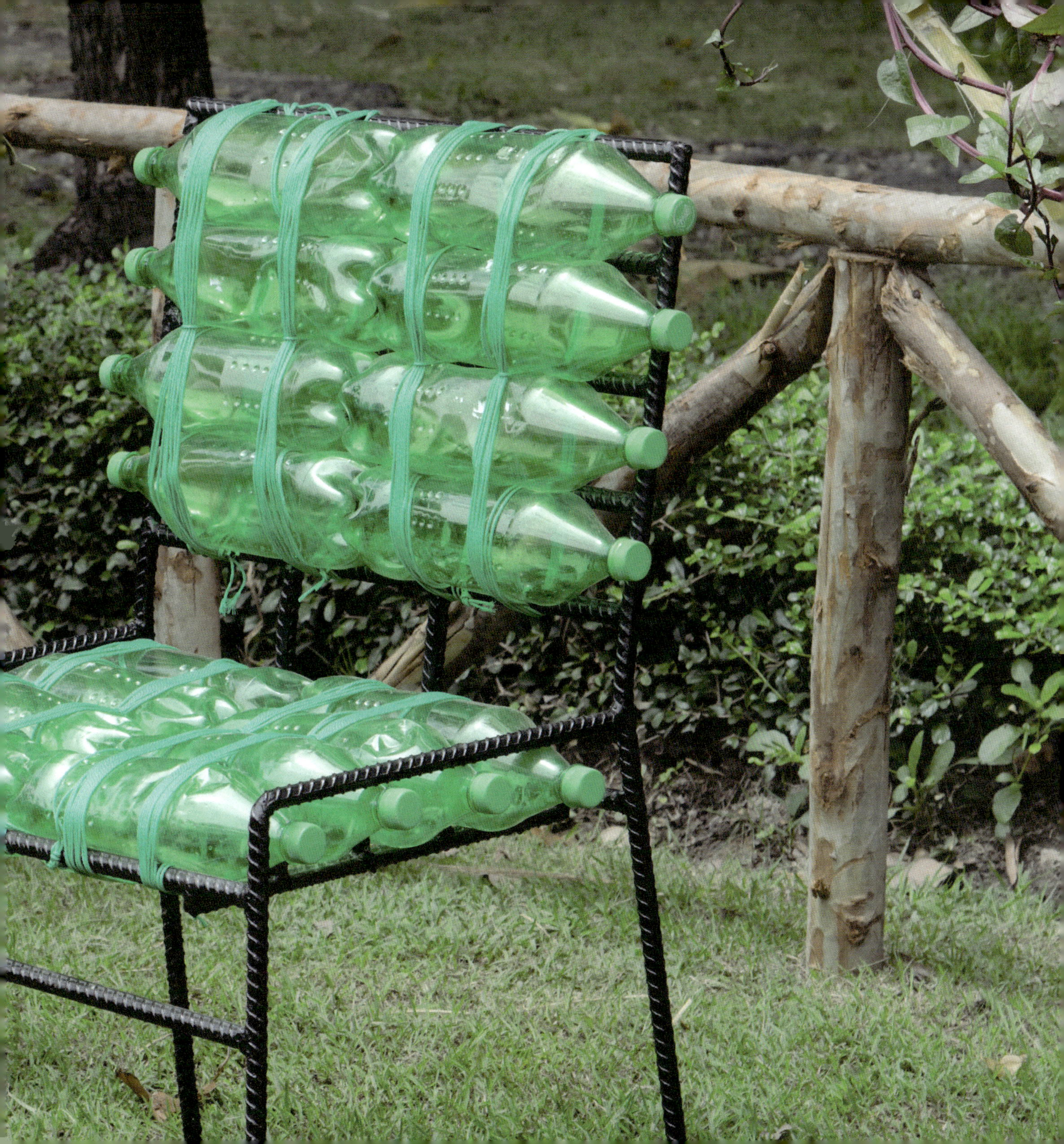

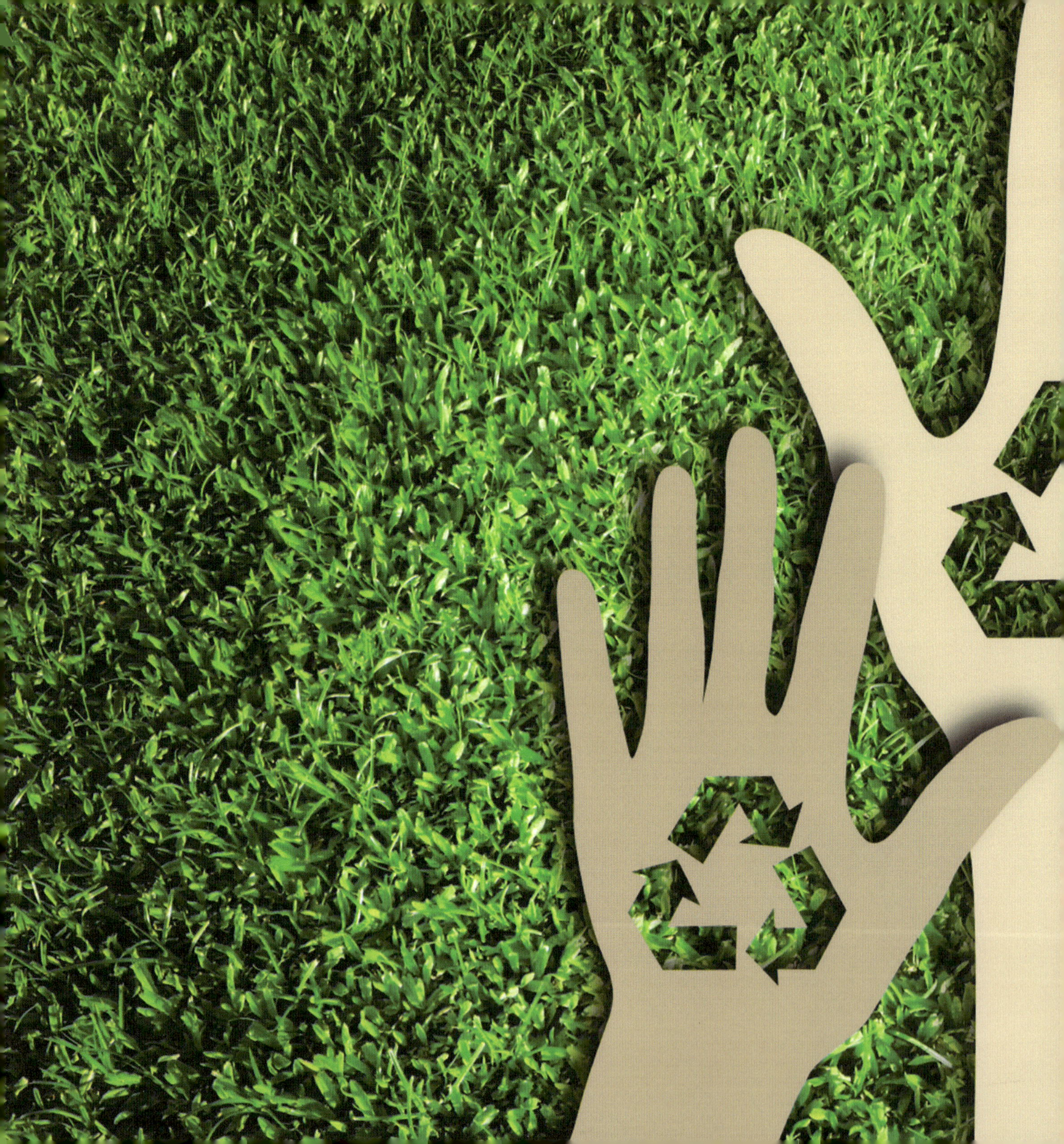

The three Rs can help conserve our natural resources. They can help minimize the landfill space we have to use for waste. The three Rs help us use less energy, emit less greenhouse gases, and contribute less to global warming.

The three Rs help us help our environment to be a safe and healthy place to live in. You can do your part now!

Reduce
Reuse
Recycle

Printed in Great Britain
by Amazon